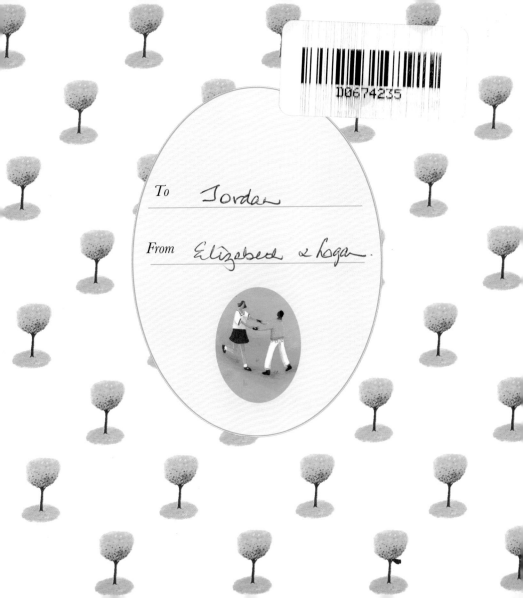

To Jordan

From Elizabeth & Logan.

Text by Lois Rock
This edition copyright © 1999 Lion Hudson
Illustrations copyright © 1999 Debbie Lush

The moral rights of the author and illustrator
have been asserted

A Lion Children's Book
an imprint of
Lion Hudson plc
Wilkinson House, Jordan Hill Road,
Oxford OX2 8DR, England
www.lionhudson.com
ISBN 978-0-7459-3901-8

First edition 1999
This printing August 2009
20 19 18 17 16 15 14

A catalogue record for this book is available
from the British Library

Printed and bound in Singapore
by Tien Wah Press (Pte) Ltd

The Lord's Prayer

The prayer that Jesus taught
two thousand years ago

Retold by Lois Rock
Illustrated by Debbie Lush

LION
CHILDREN'S

ABOUT THIS PRAYER

*T*he Lord's prayer was taught by a man named Jesus to his followers.

Two thousand years ago, this Jesus was born to a mother named Mary. His first cradle was a simple manger in a stable in Bethlehem. Yet ancient stories relate that an angel had told Mary that her child was the Son of God, and that angels sang in the skies above Bethlehem on the night that he was born.

When Jesus grew to be a man, he became much talked about in the villages around his home. Many claimed that he could work miracles, healing people with a touch. He was also a great storyteller, and crowds gathered to listen to him.

One story he told was about a father who had two sons. Together, they farmed the land to make their living.

The younger son had dreams of living a more exciting life on his own.

One day, he claimed his share of the family money and went to a distant land. There, he spent all he had on the glamorous things that money can buy.

Then famine struck. Soon, the young man had no money. He had to take a job minding a herd of pigs, and he was so hungry he wished he could eat the pigs' food.

Sad and dejected, he made the long journey home. 'Surely my father will hire me as a servant,' he thought to himself as he travelled along.

Then he heard running. His father had seen him coming, and was running to greet him. He took him home, welcomed him back as a beloved son and gave a joyful party in celebration.

'The God who made this world is like that father,' Jesus explained to his listeners.

He said that the God of the universe longs to welcome everyone with love and laughter and he told his followers how they could speak to God in prayer, as a child speaks to a parent whom they can love and trust.

Our Father, who art in heaven,

Are we alone in a vast, spinning universe... or does someone watch over us, as a parent watches over a child?

hallowed be thy Name.

And if there is a someone,
then that Someone must be

strong,

life-giving,

gentle,

good

and loving.

Thy kingdom come,

So may goodness
and love rule
in this world.

Thy will be done,
on Earth
as it is in Heaven.

*May goodness and love rule
through all the universe, both
seen and unseen.*

Give us this day our daily bread.

May the world's people have all they need to live in simplicity and joy.

And forgive us our trespasses,

When we fail to be good
and loving,
may we be forgiven.

as we forgive
those who
trespass
against us.

When we are wronged,
may we learn to forgive.

And lead us not into temptation,

May we never fall prey to hatred,
greed and wickedness.

but deliver us
from evil:

*May we be safe from
anything that might
dishearten or destroy us.*

For thine is the kingdom, the power
and the glory, for ever and ever. Amen.